How We Use

Water

Carol Ballard

www.raintreepublishers.co.uk
Visit our website to find out more information about **Raintree** books.

To order:
☎ Phone 44 (0) 1865 888112
▤ Send a fax to 44 (0) 1865 314091
▢ Visit the Raintree bookshop at **www.raintreepublishers.co.uk** to browse our catalogue and order online.

First published in Great Britain by Raintree,
Halley Court, Jordan Hill, Oxford OX2 8EJ,
part of Harcourt Education.
Raintree is a registered trademark of Harcourt
Education Ltd.

Editorial: Nick Hunter and Richard Woodham
Design: Kim Saar and Bridge Creative Services Ltd
Picture Research: Maria Joannou and Debra Weatherley
Production: Amanda Meaden
Indexing: Indexing Specialists (UK) Ltd

Originated by Ambassador Litho Ltd
Printed and bound in Hong Kong, China by
South China Printing Company

ISBN 1 844 43441 9
09 08 07 06 05
10 9 8 7 6 5 4 3 2 1

British Library Cataloguing in Publication Data
Ballard, Carol
How We Use Water. – (Using Materials)
553.7
A full catalogue record for this book is available from the British Library.

Acknowledgements
The publishers would like to thank the following for permission to reproduce photographs: Alamy p. 13; Corbis p. 19 (Harcourt Index); Getty Images pp. 9 (Stone), 10 (Photodisc/Harcourt Index), 17 (TIB), 20 (Photodisc/Harcourt Index), 21 (Taxi), 22 (Photodisc/Harcourt Index), 23 (Imagebank), 24 (Thinkstock), 25 (Photodisc/Harcourt Index), 26 (Photodisc/Harcourt Index), 29 (Imagebank); NASA p. 4; Oxford Scientific Films pp. 8 (OKAPIA), 11 (Andrew Plumptre), 16 (Gordon Maclean), 28 (Doug Allan); Photodisc p. 15 (Harcourt Index); photographersdirect.com p. 12; photolibrary.com p. 14; Robert Harding Picture Library p. 18; Science Photo Library pp. 5 (Rod Planck), 6 (Colin Cuthbert), 7 (Colin Cuthbert), 27 (Gilbert S. Grant).

Cover photograph of melting ice cubes, reproduced with permission of Zefa.

Every effort has been made to contact copyright holders of any material reproduced in this book. Any omissions will be rectified in subsequent printings if notice is given to the publishers.

The paper used to print this book comes from sustainable resources.

Contents

Any words appearing in bold, **like this**, are explained in the Glossary.

Water and its properties

All the things we use are made from materials. Water is a material. Much of our planet is covered by water. It is in the air around us and is needed by every living thing. Without it the Earth would be a dry, dusty and dead place.

We use water every day for drinking, cooking and washing. Water helps plants to grow. Ships travel on water, carrying people and goods to different places. Water is also used to provide power and **energy**.

The Earth's oceans are easily seen from space.

Rain helps
plants to grow.

The **properties** of a material tell us what it is like.

One property of water is that it is colourless. It is also **transparent** and **odourless**. At normal temperatures water is a **liquid**, but it can also be a **solid** or a **gas**.

Don't use it!

The different properties of materials make them useful for some jobs. The properties also make them unsuitable for other jobs. For example, we don't normally use water instead of petrol in our cars. Water does not burn so it would not give the car the energy it needs.

Where does water come from?

Water is a **natural** material. About seven-tenths of the Earth's surface is covered in water. All of our oceans, rivers, lakes and puddles contain it. The ice at the North and South Poles is frozen water.

Some reservoirs are natural lakes, but others are man-made.

Water is carried underground in pipes like these.

When we turn on a tap, water comes out. It has had a long journey to get there. It begins when water flows into large lakes or **reservoirs**. It is not clean enough for us to use, so it is cleaned at a water treatment works. Dirt and **germs** are removed. When the water is clean, it is stored in large tanks. Underground pipes carry water from these tanks to the taps in homes and schools.

Solid, liquid or gas?

We usually think of water as the clear **liquid** that we use every day. Water can also be a **gas** or a **solid**. If you heat water to 100° Celsius, it boils and **evaporates**. It becomes a gas that we call **water vapour**. If you cool water to 0° Celsius, it freezes and becomes solid ice.

The water cycle

Water is being **recycled** all the time. Warmth from the Sun heats the water in seas and lakes. This makes the water **evaporate**. **Water vapour** rises high into the air. The air is colder higher up, so the water vapour cools down and turns back into tiny drops of **liquid** water. These join together to form clouds. The clouds are blown along by the wind. The water droplets then fall to the ground as rain or snow.

A snowflake is made from crystals of frozen water.

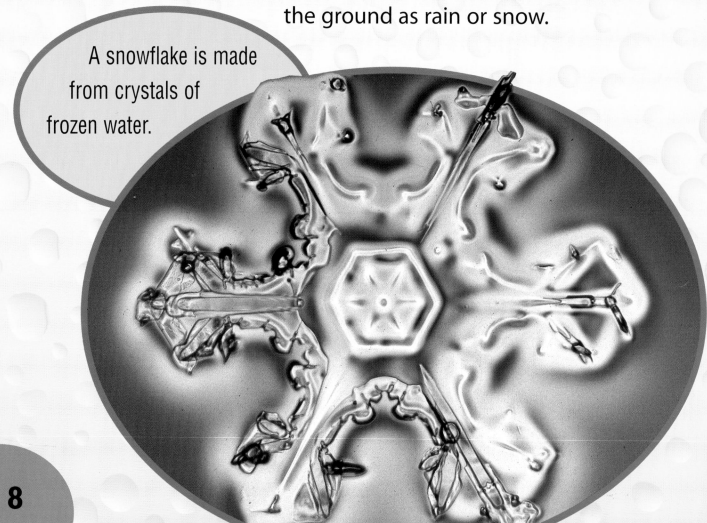

Some rivers
bend and twist along
their route to the sea.

The water collects together to form tiny streams. These join up to form larger streams and rivers. These streams and rivers lead to lakes and seas, where the whole process starts all over again! This process is called the water cycle.

Breathing out

If you breathe out on a cold morning your breath might look cloudy. This is because your breath is warm and contains water vapour. As the cold air cools your breath, the water vapour turns into tiny drops of liquid water.

Water for drinking

About three-quarters of your body is made from water. We need water to stay alive. Without water, we soon become thirsty. People who go without water for several days can become very ill. Running, cycling or dancing can make you hot and sticky. Your body loses water as you sweat. It is important to drink plenty of water to replace what you lose.

A glass of cold water is very refreshing on a hot day.

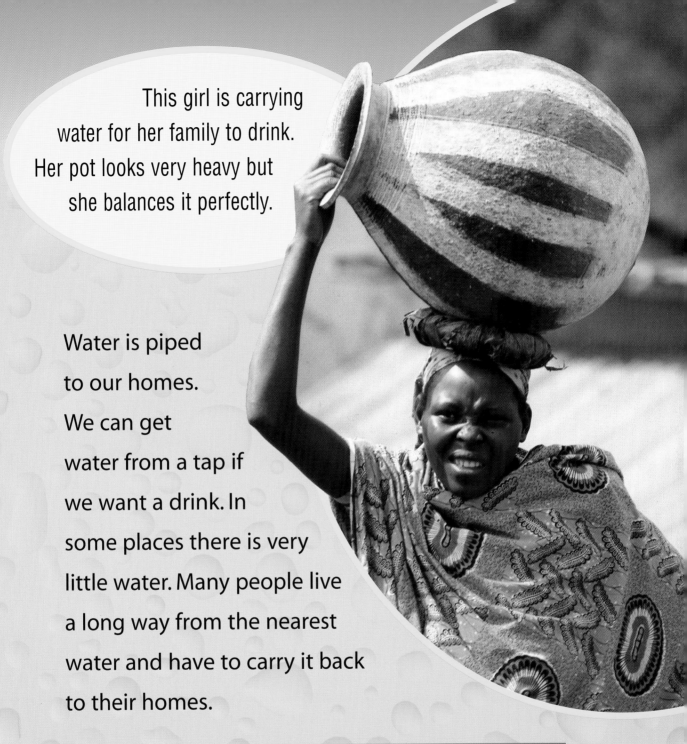

This girl is carrying water for her family to drink. Her pot looks very heavy but she balances it perfectly.

Water is piped to our homes. We can get water from a tap if we want a drink. In some places there is very little water. Many people live a long way from the nearest water and have to carry it back to their homes.

Don't use it!

Sweet fizzy drinks contain water but they often contain other things that are not good for you. Some have a lot of sugar that can cause tooth decay. Some have other **chemicals** *added. It makes sense not to drink too many of these drinks.*

Water for washing

To stay clean we need to wash ourselves and the things that we use. Water is a good material to use for washing because it is a **liquid** that does not harm our bodies. It washes dirt from our bodies and from things like dirty dishes. Water is colourless and also **odourless**, so we do not smell after we wash in it. Using soap can make things even cleaner.

Keeping clean can be fun, too!

A breezy, sunny day is best for drying the washing.

When our clothes get dirty, they need to be washed. This can be done using a washing machine. Some fabrics are **delicate** and need to be washed by hand. Plates, cutlery and saucepans all need washing after a meal. You can use a dishwasher or wash them by hand.

Don't use it!

*Some fabrics can be damaged if they get wet, so we don't use water to wash them. Dry cleaning uses special **chemicals** instead of water to remove dirt. The chemicals clean the fabric but do not damage it.*

Cars can be washed using a bucket and sponge or a hosepipe. Many petrol stations have machines that do the work for you.

Water for playing

Almost everyone likes playing in water! Water allows us to float and we can jump into it without hurting ourselves. It is a good idea to learn to swim as soon as you can, so that you can stay safe in and around water. Swimming pools are good places to improve your swimming skills.

Before you swim, check how deep the water is and look for the lifeguard.

These two children are learning how to paddle a canoe.

Snorkelling lets you see what is happening under water. Scuba divers can explore very deep water. Water sports such as windsurfing, sailing and canoeing are all good fun, too.

Taking a trip on a boat can be a good way to travel and look at the scenery. Cruise holidays on the sea or along rivers and canals are popular.

Stay safe

Playing in water is fun but it can also be dangerous. You must remember to be careful. Always obey the safety rules at a swimming pool and read warning signs at beaches. Never swim on your own and only use those places which are meant for water sports.

Water for growing

All living things need water. Plants need water to grow. Most plants have roots that hold them firmly in the soil. Among other things, the roots **absorb** water from the soil and carry it to the other parts of the plant.

Plants in tubs and baskets often need to be watered every day in hot, dry weather.

Plants that grow in hot, dry places need to save as much water as they can.

Farmers need to water large fields of crops. They use water pipes with pumps and sprinklers attached. These can spray water over whole fields.

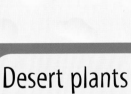

Desert plants

Deserts are very dry places so anything living there has to be able to survive with very little water. The thick stems of cacti store water and their roots spread out just below the ground so they can absorb any water that falls.

Moving water

Because water is a **liquid**, it can be poured. Wherever you put water, it will spread out to take the shape of its container. Water always flows downhill. Water flows in a gentle trickle in a small mountain stream. In large rivers there is often a strong **force** called a **current**.

The force of these waves is enough to wear away the rocky cliffs.

The energy in moving water keeps a surfer on his board.

The movement of water downhill creates a force. We can use the force of moving water in many ways to create **energy**.

Tides

The water in seas and oceans is not still. Winds and currents make water rise and fall in waves. These can be small and gentle or strong and wild. Twice a day, the water in seas and oceans creeps closer to the shore. Twice a day it slips back away from the shore. These movements are called tides.

Water for energy

People have used water to make things work for thousands of years. Water mills have a large water wheel. The **energy** in moving water turns the water wheel. This then turns other wheels, which can pump water or work machines.

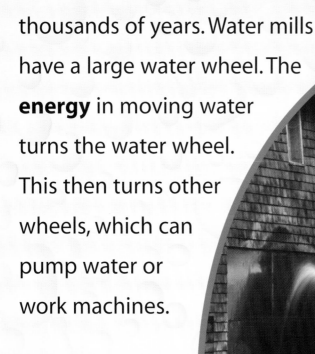

Water mills like this had many uses, including grinding grain for making bread.

Steam engines were used to pull trains carrying people and goods.

Water can be used to make electricity. Dams are built on rivers to hold water back. When it is allowed through it flows downhill to a power station. Here, it turns wheels called **turbines**. These turn the **generators** which make electricity. The movement of tides and waves can be used in the same way.

Steam engines

Steam engines *can be used to work many machines. If water is heated, it boils and turns to a gas called* ***water vapour****. This needs more space than liquid water and will push on its container. This* ***force*** *can push a slide called a* ***piston*** *outwards. The piston slides back in when the steam escapes. This action can make other parts move and turn.*

Water for transport

Water can be used to move things from one place to another. Some materials can float on water. Boats float because they are lighter than the water that would fill the same space. Boats have been used by people for many thousands of years.

Cargo ships transport large, heavy goods around the world.

Cruise ships take holidaymakers all over the world.

Small boats can transport people and goods on calm water such as rivers. Larger boats are needed to travel across rough seas and oceans. These boats carry passengers and goods around the world.

Canals are man-made waterways. They were built so boats could travel where there were no rivers. Today we have motorways, railways and aeroplanes but the heaviest loads can still be carried on water.

Moving logs

When trees are cut down, they have to be moved to factories and paper mills. The logs are very heavy and difficult to move. In many places, they are pulled to a river and tied together to make a raft. This can then be floated on the water and guided downstream to wherever the logs are needed.

Water for cooling

On a hot day, splashing cold water over ourselves is a great way to cool off. One **property** of water is that it can **absorb** heat but still feel cool. Water also does not **conduct** heat well. Car engines and machines in factories can be cooled down using cold water. Adding ice cubes to a **liquid** will cool the liquid down.

Ice lollies are made by freezing water that contains **flavourings**.

Firefighters are trained to put out big fires like this one.

A fire needs heat to start. If heat is removed from a burning fire, the fire will go out. Putting water on a fire lowers the temperature enough to put it out. Firefighters often use water to put out big fires.

Don't use it!
Putting water on some fires can be very dangerous. NEVER put water on burning fat or oil – water and fat don't mix and the fire will spread further. NEVER put water on an electrical fire – water can conduct electricity and you could get a dangerous electric shock.

Water for living in

Water is home to many plants and creatures. Seas and oceans contain salt water but most rivers, lakes and streams contain fresh water. Some living things are suited to salt water while others are suited to fresh water.

Fish spend all their time in water. They use their **gills** to get oxygen from the water. Their fins and tails help them to swim.

Coral reefs provide shelter for fish and other small creatures.

Jellyfish use their tentacles to sting their prey.

Animals such as frogs lay their eggs in water. These hatch into tadpoles, which grow into adult frogs. When they are fully grown, they move on to land. Other animals, like turtles, move easily between land and water. They can only breathe air, so they need to come to the water's surface regularly.

Breathing under water

Humans cannot live in water. We can only breathe air. If we stay under water too long, our lungs fill with water and we drown. When divers go under water, they have to take air in a special tank on their backs.

Water and the environment

Water controls where animals and plants can live. It also affects people's lives. Too much or too little rain can cause many problems. If a lot of rain falls in a short time, rivers may overflow. Water spills on to the land and ruins crops. Buildings can be damaged and people may be left homeless.

In some countries, rain may not fall for many months. During **droughts**, crops become weak and die. Animals and people run out of food. Without emergency help they may starve.

Very few living things can survive a long drought.

Most animals and plants cannot survive in polluted water like this.

Water may become **polluted** if people are careless with oil, **chemicals**, dirt and rubbish. These can harm everything that lives in the water. Cleaning up can take a long time and be very expensive.

Controlling floods

*Some rivers **flood** regularly, so people are prepared for this. Dams have been built to control the floodwater. In other places, **flood barriers** have been built. Dams and barriers do stop floods, but they may affect animals and plants that live in the rivers.*

Find out for yourself

The best way to find out more about water is to investigate it for yourself. Look around your home for water being used, and keep an eye out for water during your day. You will find the answers to many of your questions in this book. You can also look in other books and on the Internet.

Books to read

Science Answers: Grouping Materials, Carol Ballard (Heinemann Library, 2003)

Discovering Science: Matter, Rebecca Hunter (Raintree, 2003)

Science in Nature: The Water Cycle, Theresa Greenaway (Hodder Wayland, 2001)

Using the Internet

Try searching the Internet to find out about water. Websites can change, so if some of the links below no longer work, don't worry. Use a search engine such as www.yahooligans.com or www.internet4kids.com. You could try searching using the keywords 'water cycle', 'drought' and 'flood'. Here are some websites to get you started.

Websites

A great site, which explains all about different materials:
http://www.bbc.co.uk/schools/revisewise/science/materials/

Everything you could want to know about water:
http://www.thinkquest.org/library/site_sum.html?tname=C0115522&url=C0115522/

Glossary

absorb soak up liquid

chemical substance that we use to make other substances, or for jobs such as cleaning

conduct carry or transmit heat or electricity

current flow of something, for example, a river

delicate easily damaged

desert place where there is very little rain

drought time when no rain falls

energy power to do work

evaporate when liquid water turns into a gas called water vapour

flavourings substance added to a food or drink to give it a certain taste

flood water spilling over land

flood barrier barrier put up to stop floodwater coming on to land

force push or a pull

gas something in a state where it spreads out into all the space it can

generator part of a power station that makes electricity

germ tiny living thing that can make you ill

gills part of a fish's body that takes in oxygen from water

liquid something in a runny state that can be poured from one container to another

natural anything that is not made by people

odourless has no smell

piston part of an engine

polluted spoilt, dirty or impure

property characteristic or quality of a material

recycle use again

reservoir lake for storing water

snorkel tube that lets you breathe as you swim under water

solid having a fixed shape and size

steam engine engine driven by heating water

transparent something we can see through clearly

turbine part of the machinery at a power station

water vapour gas that water turns into when it boils and evaporates

Index

Titles in the *Using Materials* series include:

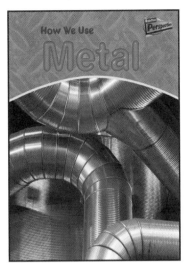

Hardback   1 844 43436 2

Hardback   1 844 43437 0

Hardback   1 844 43438 9

Hardback   1 844 43439 7

Hardback   1 844 43440 0

Hardback   1 844 43441 9

Find out about the other titles in this series on our website www.raintreepublishers.co.uk